Hide and Seek

PROGRAM AUTHORS
Richard L. Allington
Ronald L. Cramer
Patricia M. Cunningham
G. Yvonne Pérez
Constance Frazier Robinson
Robert J. Tierney

PROGRAM CONSULTANTS   **CRITIC READERS**
Bernadine J. Bolden   Maria P. Barela
Ann Hall   Phinnize J. Brown
Sylvia M. Lee   Jean C. Carter
Dolores Perez   Nancy Peterson
Jo Ann Wong   Nancy Welsh

John C. Manning, *Instructional Consultant*

SCOTT, FORESMAN AND COMPANY
Editorial Offices: Glenview, Illinois

Regional Sales Offices: Palo Alto, California •
Tucker, Georgia • Glenview, Illinois •
Oakland, New Jersey • Dallas, Texas

ACKNOWLEDGMENTS

Text

The second stanza of "Let's Pretend" from *A World to Know* by James S. Tippett. Copyright 1933 by Harper & Brothers, renewed 1961 by Martha K. Tippett. Reprinted by permission of Harper & Row, Publishers, Inc.

Christina Rossetti, "Mix a Pancake" from *Sing Song,* 1872.

"I Held a Lamb" by Kim Worthington from *Child Life.* Copyright 1954 by Child Life, Inc. Reprinted by permission.

"The Snake" from *Dogs and Dragons, Trees and Dreams* by Karla Kuskin. Copyright © 1958 by Karla Kuskin. Reprinted by permission of Harper & Row, Publishers, Inc.

"I Wouldn't" from *You Read to Me, I'll Read to You* by John Ciardi. Copyright © 1962 by John Ciardi. Reprinted by permission of Harper & Row, Publishers, Inc.

Photographs

Page 149 (top): *Say Hello, Vanessa* by Marjorie Weinman Sharmat. Holiday House, 1979; Page 149 (middle): *Toby in the Country, Toby in the City* by Maxine Zohn Bozzo. Greenwillow Books, 1982; Page 149 (bottom): *Little Black Bear Goes for a Walk* by Berniece Freschet. Charles Scribner's Sons, 1977.

Artists

Blake, Gerrie 10–15; Brooks, David 121; Brooks, Nan 16–21; Craig, John 36–46; Delacre, Lulu 102–106; Miyake, Yoshi 108–109, 110–115, 116–120; Freshman, Shelley 52–56; Iosa, Ann 22–23; Kock, Carl 58–59, 60–65, 66–71; Lazarevich, Mila 50; Lizak, Laura 48; Marable, Julie 124–125, 126–133; Munger, Nancy 88–89, 95–100; Neill, Eileen Mueller 24–28, 90–94, 122–123; Nelson Anita 134, 135–139; Pate, Rodney 72–85; Randstrom, Susan 101; Sanford, John 140–147; Sumichrast, Josef 8–9; Temz, Reya 29–34; Wilson, Don 7, 35, 57, 107, 148, 150–158

Freelance Photographs

Susan Friedman Photography 47–49, 51

Cover Artist

Don Wilson

Contents

Stories by:

Beverly Keller

Marjorie Meyer

DuPage Learning Systems, Inc.

Sallie Runck

Making Friends

Lost and Found

The Puppy Who Ran

Jake has a puppy.
The puppy's name is Panda.
Jake and Panda like to go to
the park and play.

One day on the way to the park, Jake
and Panda saw two fire trucks go by.
Panda did not like them and ran fast!

Panda stopped by the lake.

"Where am I?" she said.

A frog came jumping from the lake.

The puppy said, "My name is Panda,
and I am lost."

The frog said, "My name is Frog.
Where do you live, Panda?"

"I live in a blue house," Panda said.
"It is a long way from here."

"What is your house number, Panda?" Frog asked.

"What is a house number?" Panda said.

"With no house number, you are lost!" Frog said.

The puppy said, "I lost Jake too."

"Jake who?" Frog asked as he jumped at a fly.

Panda said, "Jake, that is all."

"Jake is a first name!" Frog said.
"Who can find a boy with one name?"

Panda was not happy at all, and so
she said, "Tell me what I can do."

"You said you live a long way from
here," Frog said.

"I live right by a park," Panda said.

Frog jumped up.
"If we can find where that park is,
we can look for that blue house!"

They walked and jumped a long way.

When they came to a big park,
Panda said, "That park is the one!
That blue house is where I live!"

"We are on Park Way," Frog said.
"And a number four is on that door.
You live at Number Four Park Way."

"I will get that number right!"
Panda said.
"It is not funny for me to be lost.
But if I can tell the right name and
number, I will not be lost for long."

"So long," Frog said.

"So long, you good old frog!"
Panda said.

Frog went jumping to the lake, and
Panda ran to Jake.

Ellie Plays a Joke

"Take Ellie to the park with you," Mother said to Bill.
"I have to go see Mrs. Green."

"Why do I have to take my little sister?" Bill asked.

Mother just said, "Ellie, go with Bill."

So Ellie went with Bill to the park.
Mother went to see Mrs. Green.

"Will you play ball with me?"
Ellie asked Bill.

"Play ball with my little sister?
What a joke!" Bill said.
"You just play around here now."

Bill saw two big boys in the park.
He went to play ball with them.

"I'll play a joke," Ellie said, and
she ran when Bill was not looking.

"I can play a good joke!" Ellie said.
"I'll hide in this funny old boat so
Bill has to find me."

Ellie jumped into the boat to hide.
When the big boys went to eat, Bill
looked around.

"Where did my sister go?" Bill said.
"Are you playing a joke on me, Ellie?
Do not hide from me."

Bill looked all around the park.

"If my sister is not around here, she has to be at the house," Bill said.

Bill ran all the way to the house.

"My sister is not here," he said. "Now I have to tell Mother I lost my sister!"

Bill started out for Mrs. Green's house to tell Mother he lost Ellie.

By now, Ellie was out of the boat.

She said, "A joke is not funny when
you have to hide too long."

But now Bill was not around!
Ellie looked all around the park.

"Why did I hide?" Ellie said.
"I have to tell Mother I lost Bill."

Ellie started out for Mrs. Green's
house to tell Mother she lost Bill.

Just when Bill came to Mrs. Green's house, he saw Ellie.

"Ellie! Ellie!" Bill called.
"I lost you in the park."

Ellie ran to Bill and said, "I went to hide in a boat, and I lost you! It was not a funny joke to hide."

"It is all right now," Bill said.
"We can go to the park and play ball now—but no jokes!"

Let's Make Believe

Baby Bear at School

School was out for the day.
No one was around to read the
books on the table.

Baby Bear in <u>The Three Bears</u> book
said, "The boys and girls have
fun here at school.
I want to have fun at school too.
I'll just step out of my book."

Baby Bear stepped out of the book.

Now Baby Bear was big!
He walked to the back of the room.
He stepped on a rope.

Baby Bear looked at the rope and
said, "The boys and girls jump rope.
I'll jump rope too."

He started to jump rope.

"Jumping rope is too hard for
me," said Baby Bear.
"I keep stepping on the rope.
I'll put the rope next to this boat."

Next Baby Bear saw a ball.

He said, "The boys and girls have
fun when they catch the ball.
I'll catch the ball too."

Baby Bear started to catch the ball.

Then he said, "Catching the ball is
too hard for me.
I have to move too fast to catch it.
I'll put it next to this house."

Next Baby Bear saw a truck.
He started to make it go fast.
A chair was in the way.
Baby Bear wanted to turn the truck.
He turned and turned, but he did
not turn the truck in time.
It ran into the chair and stopped.

"Turning the truck is too hard for
me," said Baby Bear.
"School is not fun for a little bear.
I'll step back into my book."

The next day at school a boy asked,
"Did you move the truck here?"

A girl asked, "What went on here?
I can not find the ball.
And where is the jump rope?"

That was funny to Baby Bear.
But he did not laugh.
He just looked happy to be back in
The Three Bears book.

Going to the Zoo

One day Mary and Sam went next door to Sue's house.

Sue said, "We can go to the zoo. We can see an elephant and a wolf and a turtle at the zoo."

Mary, Sam, and Sue stepped out of the house behind Sue's father. Just then it started to rain.

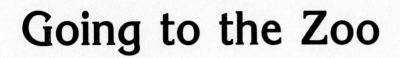

"It is raining hard," said Father.
"We can not go to the zoo when
it is raining this hard."

"If it is raining too hard, we can
play here," said Sue.

Sue's mother said, "Come back
here with me.
You can play back here.
This is a good room to play in
when it is raining."

"What a room!" said Mary.
"We can dress up like zoo animals.
Look at this big old coat and the
shoes behind it.
I'll dress up in the coat and shoes.
I'll look like an elephant."

Sue said, "You need what is behind
this chair too.
Now you will look like an elephant.
But what can I put on?
I want to dress up too."

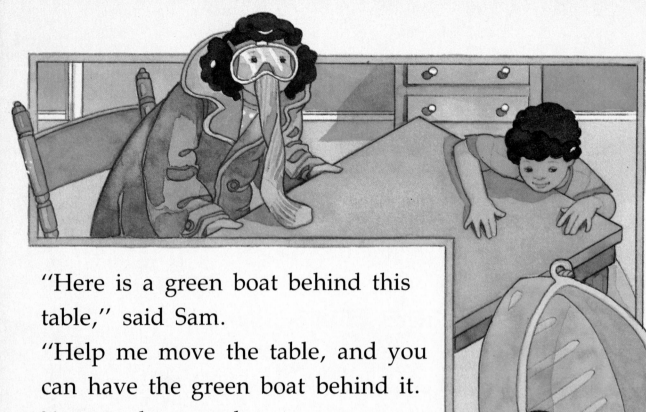

"Here is a green boat behind this table," said Sam.
"Help me move the table, and you can have the green boat behind it.
You can be a turtle.
Now all you need are four shoes."

Sue said, "I see some old shoes.
Here, Mary, catch the shoes."

Sam said, "You are a funny turtle.
Now it is my turn to dress up.
I want to dress up like a wolf.
Help me find a coat and shoes."

"This coat behind the door will be just right for a wolf," said Sue. "I do not see shoes, but here, catch this hat."

Sam put on the coat and hat and said, "I am a wolf.
I move like a wolf.
Step back out of my way!"

"You are not a wolf," said Mary.
"I am not going to move.
You are just Sam dressed up in a big old coat and hat!"

Sam said, "When I move around in this big old coat, I get too hot."

Just then Sue's mother came to the door and said, "It stopped raining. Do you want to go to the zoo?"

"Yes!" said Sue and Mary.

"Yes!" said Sam.
"It is not fun to be dressed up like a wolf.
But it will be fun to see one!"

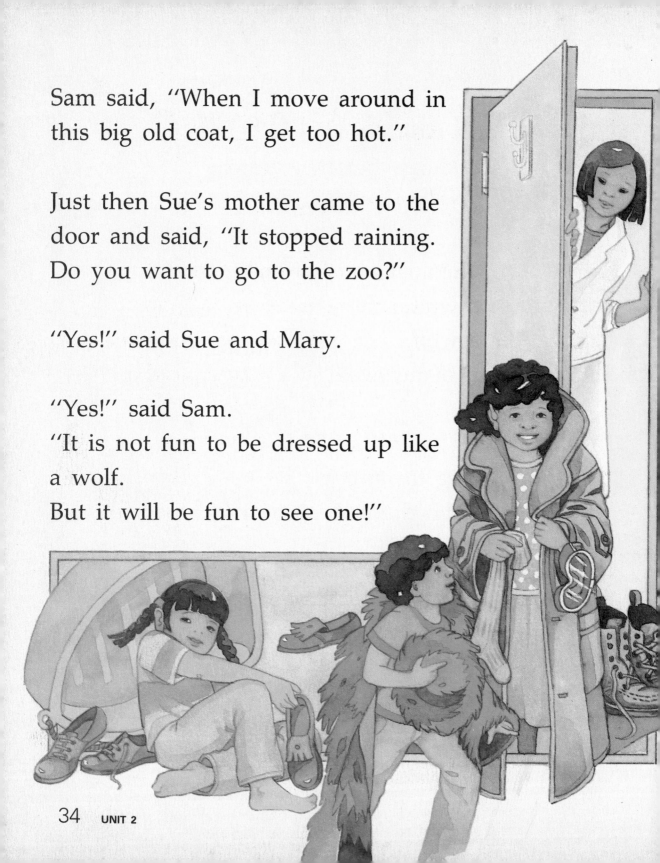

Let's Pretend

by James S. Tippett

Let's pretend we're elephants
Who trample down tall grass,
Who force their way through jungles
And trumpet as they pass.

35

Bake It —Make It

The Gingerbread Man

In this play are:

WOMAN   **MAN**   **GINGERBREAD MAN**   **FOX**

The **STORYTELLER** reads from The Gingerbread Man.

STORYTELLER: A woman and a man
  lived far, far back in time.
  The woman lived in a red house.
  The man lived in the house too.
  A fox lived not far from them.
  He lived in a yellow house.

WOMAN (taking out a pan): I will make a gingerbread cake for us.

STORYTELLER: The woman made the cake look like a gingerbread man. She made a little blue coat for the gingerbread man. Next she made little tan shoes. Then she made a little red hat.

WOMAN (putting the cake in to bake): I know I have made a good gingerbread man for us.

STORYTELLER: By and by she looked in at the gingerbread man. Just then he jumped out of the pan and ran out the door.

GINGERBREAD MAN (turning his head and calling back): Run, run as fast as you can. You can not catch me. I am the gingerbread man!

WOMAN (running after GINGERBREAD MAN): Stop, gingerbread man, stop!

STORYTELLER: The woman moved fast, but she did not catch the gingerbread man.
The woman was far, far behind.

The man was planting some seeds.
He saw the woman running after the gingerbread man.

GINGERBREAD MAN (turning his head and calling back): Run, run as fast as you can.
You can not catch me.
I am the gingerbread man!

MAN (taking his pail and running after GINGERBREAD MAN): Stop, gingerbread man, stop!
Do not run from us!
Come back to us!

STORYTELLER: The man moved fast, but he did not catch the gingerbread man.

The man was far, far behind.

After that, the woman and the man went back to the red house where they lived.

WOMAN: He moved too fast for us.

MAN: Yes, he moved too fast for us.

STORYTELLER: Next the gingerbread man ran by the fox's house. The fox was hiding behind his yellow house.

GINGERBREAD MAN: I see you. I know you are hiding from me.

FOX: No, I am not hiding from you.

GINGERBREAD MAN (turning his head and calling back): Run, run as fast as you can. You can not catch me. I am the gingerbread man!

FOX: I do not want to run after you.

STORYTELLER: Just then the gingerbread man came to a lake.

FOX: I will give you a ride. Just jump on my back.

GINGERBREAD MAN (jumping on FOX's back): Where are you going?

FOX: The water is getting on you. Jump on my head.

GINGERBREAD MAN (jumping on FOX's head): I want to know where you are going.

FOX (laughing): You will see.

GINGERBREAD MAN: Now I know why you did not run after me. Now I know you are playing a joke on me.

FOX: I know I am going to eat you!

A Puppet to Make

This girl makes puppets.
She made a gingerbread man puppet.
She moved his head around.
She made the puppet look as if he
was talking.

You can make a gingerbread man
puppet too.

Here is what you need to make your gingerbread man puppet.

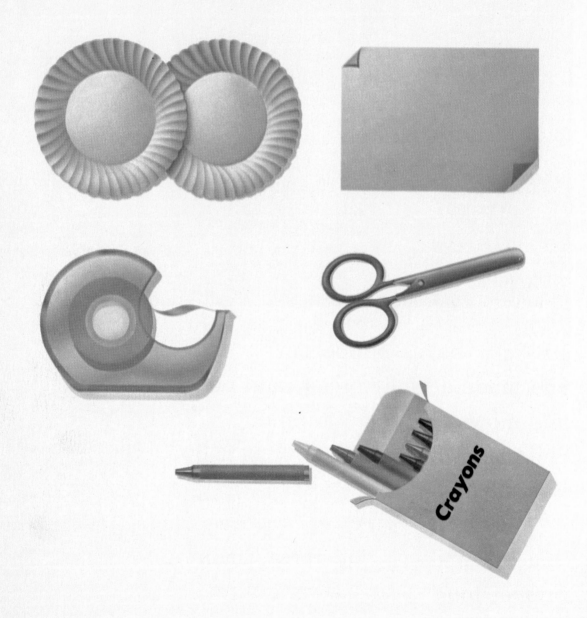

Here is what you do.

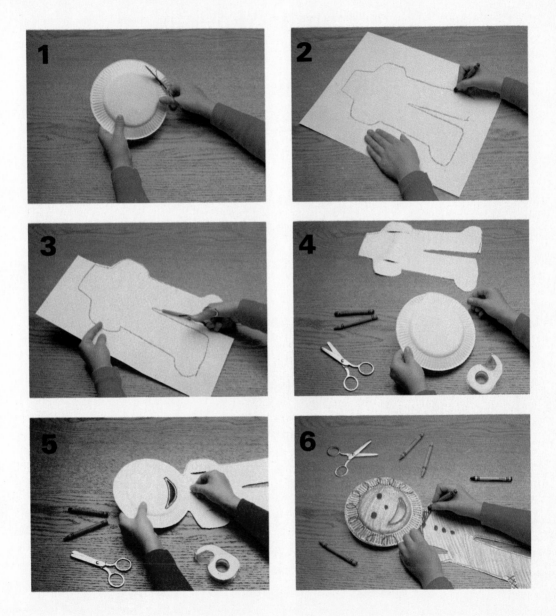

Make your puppet move around.

To be read
by the teacher

Mix a Pancake

by Christina Rossetti

Mix a pancake,
Stir a pancake,
   Pop it in the pan;
Fry the pancake,
Toss the pancake,—
   Catch it if you can.

You can make this.
You can put it in a book
where you stop reading.

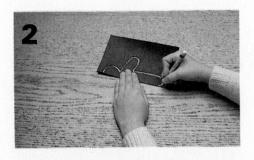

The Boy Who Called "Wolf!"

A boy looked after his father's
animals in sun and in rain.

The boy said, "I keep my father's
animals from getting lost.
I keep a wolf from coming
around them.

But it is the same, day after day,
sitting here looking after
my father's animals.
For a laugh, I'll play a joke."

"Help!" the boy called.
"Here comes a wolf!"

Girl and woman, man and boy
all came running.
But no wolf was around.

That was so funny to the boy
that he made a game of it.

Day after day, he called, "Help! Here comes a wolf!"

Day after day, girl and woman, man and boy all ran to help. The boy laughed at them, day after day.

Then one day, the boy saw a wolf hiding not far from the animals. Just the look of the wolf made the boy want to turn and run!

"Help!" he called.
"A wolf is here!"

No one ran to help.

"That boy needs a new joke,"
a woman said.

"<u>Help</u>!" the boy called.
"The wolf is right here!"

No one came.

A man laughed.
"He can not play a joke on us with
that same old game," he said.

The boy ran to a house for help.
But it did no good, for by now
the wolf was taking the animals.

**If you keep telling what is not so,
no one can know when you are
telling what is so.**

Section Two
Going Places

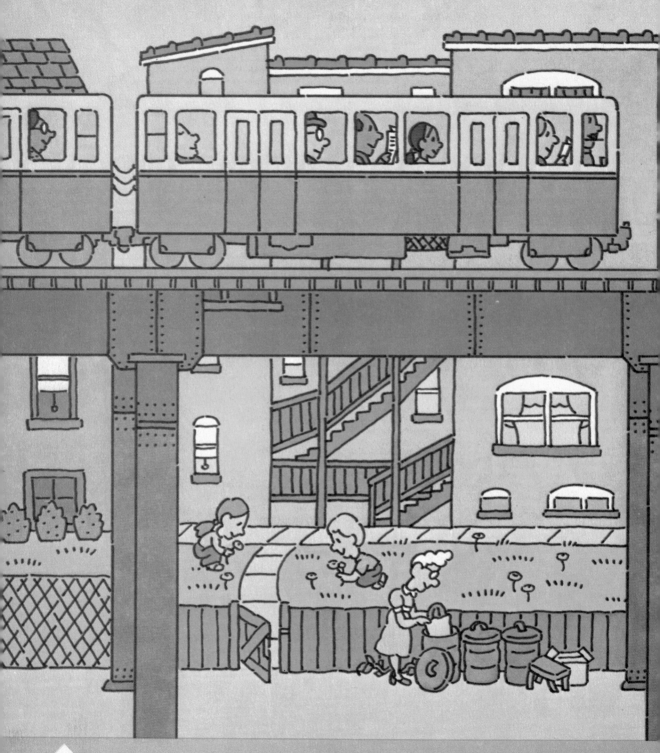

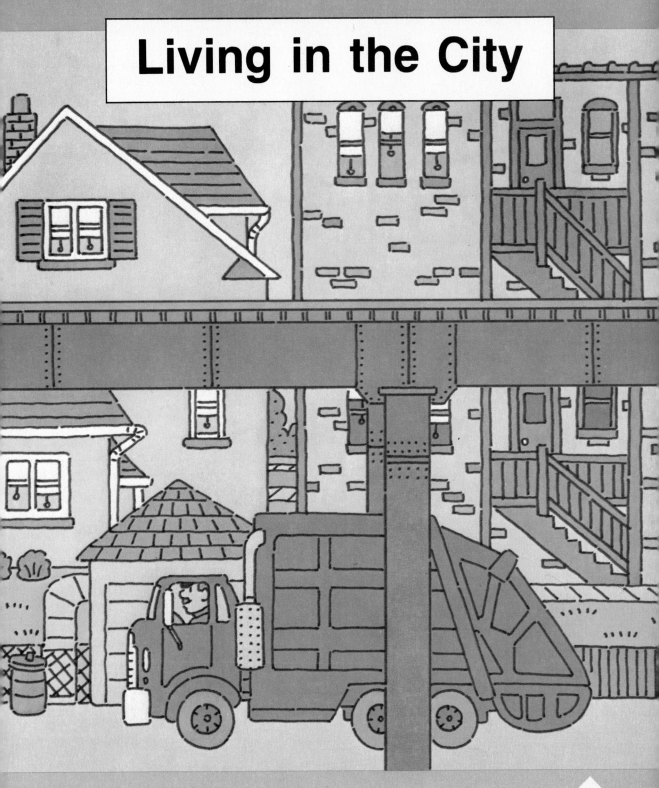

Living in the City

Something
Next to the Cans

Mother said, "Rita, here is an old
chair, which I do not want.
Please take it out to the cans."

"I'll take it now," said Rita.

Rita saw something little and green
next to the cans.

Rita called, "Tom, please come here!
I have something to show you."

"You have something to show me,"
said Tom, running to Rita.
"What is it?"

"Do you see this vine?" asked Rita.
"If the vine lives, we can have
something good to eat."

Tom said, "But little children will
find the vine and play with it."

Rita said, "We can keep the vine a
secret from the little children.
I'll put this chair on the vine.
Can you see the vine now?"

Tom said, "No, but a truck will
come to pick up what is in the cans.
The chair will be picked up too.
Then the vine will not be a secret
from the little children."

Rita said, "I know Mr. Cole, the
man on the truck.
I'll show the vine to Mr. Cole."

When the truck came, Rita said,
"Mr. Cole, the chair is hiding
something from the little children.
Please help us keep it a secret."

Rita picked up the chair and showed
the vine to Mr. Cole.

"Why, it is a melon vine!" he said.
"I see three melons on the vine.
I do not need to take the chair
along this time.
Just put it back."

The days went by.
The little children did not find
the vine.
Tom and Rita watered the vine.
The sun helped the melons on the
secret vine get big.

One day Rita and Tom showed the
melons to Mr. Cole.

"They are big now," said Mr. Cole.
"You can pick them."

Rita said to Mr. Cole, "Please take a melon for helping us keep a secret. Please show us which one you want."

Mr. Cole said, "Rita and Tom, which melons do you children want?"

Rita picked the melon she wanted, which was a green and yellow one. Tom picked the melon he wanted, which was all green. Then Mr. Cole picked his melon.

"I like melons," Mr. Cole said. "I like keeping secrets too."

The Flying Melon

Mother was taking Rita to see Aunt
Carla and Uncle Luis.
It was time to go to the train.

"I'll get my melon to take to Aunt
Carla and Uncle Luis," said Rita.
"Can Tom come along with us?
He wants to ride on the train too."

Mother said, "Tom, go ask if you
can come along on the train."

Tom came back and said, "I can go along to see your aunt and uncle."

So Rita's mother and the two children started down the steps.
Taffy, Tom's puppy, was on the steps.
Taffy jumped up on Rita and started to lick the melon.

"No, Taffy!" said Rita as the melon went flying down the steps.

Taffy started to chase the melon.
But it went down too fast for Taffy.
Rita chased the melon.
But it went down too fast for Rita.
Tom chased the melon.
But it went down too fast for Tom.

Then Taffy stopped chasing the melon.
And Rita stopped chasing it.
And Tom stopped chasing it.

The melon went all the way down.
When it stopped, it was not a big
melon.

Taffy started to eat the melon.

Mother said, "Please stop, Taffy.
The melon can make you sick."

Rita said, "My big melon is no good.
Now I have no melon to take to
Aunt Carla and Uncle Luis!"

Tom said, "Taffy can not go along
on the train.
So I'll put Taffy in my room.
Then I'll get my melon, which you
can take to your aunt and uncle."

After Tom came back, Mother, Rita,
and Tom went to the train.

The train came along.
Mother and the children stepped
on the train and sat down.

"Please let me take the melon now,
Tom," said Rita.
"I will not let it go this time."

"No, please do not," said Mother.
"We want Aunt Carla and Uncle
Luis to have this melon."

Working and Playing

Starting to Skate

Tim said, "Aunt Fay and I are going to the city to skate now. Can you come along, Joe?"

Joe said, "My dad said I can come along."

"I like going to the city, but I am not good at skating."

Tim said, "We can skate together.
I'll keep us both up.
If we fall, we will fall together."

So Tim and Joe went to the city
with Aunt Fay.
The two children skated together.
Joe started to fall down.
Tim did not let Joe fall.

When it was lunch time, Aunt Fay
said, "Do both of you like pizza?"

"Do we both like pizza!" said Tim.
"Pizza is just the thing we like!"

"Then we will have pizza for lunch,"
said Aunt Fay.
"I'll find out what things we can get
on the pizza.
Then you can tell me which two
things you want."

Just then the boys saw Aunt Fay's
hat fall.
It started to blow away.

"I must get my hat," said Aunt Fay.
"I do not want it to blow away."

She skated after the red hat.
But it was blowing away fast.
It started blowing by Tim.
He skated after it too.

But then the red hat started blowing
along by Joe.

Joe wanted to get it.
He skated with little steps.
He went this way and that way.
Then he started moving along.
Joe was skating!

Joe skated after the red hat.
It was not blowing so fast now.
Joe picked up the hat.

Joe skated to Aunt Fay.
He gave the red hat to Tim's aunt.

"Thank you, Joe!" she said.
"You stopped my hat from blowing.
That was good skating!"

"Thanks," said Joe.
"I can skate now!"

Aunt Fay said, "We can eat lunch.
You can have all the things you
want on the pizza!"

Going to Work in the City

It was a big day for Kim.
She was going to the city to see
what both Mom and Dad did at work.
They sat together on the train.

"I like to work," said Kim.
"I want to help you both work."

When the train stopped in the city,
Mom, Dad, and Kim stepped out.

Mom went to where she worked.
Kim went to work with Dad.
They met a woman.

She said, "I just lost a ring that my
father gave me.
It must be around here."

Just then Kim saw something little
fall from the woman's dress.

"This must be the ring," said Kim.

"Thank you!" said the woman.

Then Kim and Dad met a big girl.

The girl said, "Please help me.
I was taking little Benny for a walk.
Along the way I met a girl I know.
After we met, we talked a long time.
Benny must have run away.
Now I must find little Benny."

Kim gave the girl a chair.
Dad called the lost children's rooms.
Little Benny was in one of them!

"Thank you," said the girl.

Dad said, "It is time to eat, Kim."

Kim and Dad met Mom for lunch.

After lunch Mom said, "Now I'll
show Kim where I work."

Kim went to work with Mom.

Kim met a man coming in the door.

The man said, "Please help me find a good book for little children."

Kim gave the man a train book.
She gave the man a bear book.
She gave the man a puppet book.

"Thank you," said the man.
"The children I am getting a book for will like this thick train book."

Kim walked away to go help Mom.

Mom said, "Some new books came.
I must put them away."

"Can both of us do it?" asked Kim.

"Yes, thank you, Kim," said Mom.
"We can work together.
I'll show you what to do."

Kim said, "I like coming to work
with you and Dad.
I can help both of you work."

Here is something
you can
eat for lunch.

1. Get some bread like this.

2. Then you must get the things you see here.

3. Put the things together on the bread.

Now you can start eating!

Country Ways

A Fine Ride

Jill sat down in the school bus.
She sat next to Betty.

"This bus is hot," said Jill.

The bus started to go.

"I wish this bus did not shake,"
said Jill.

Soon the bus stopped for some sheep.

"This bus is slow," said Jill.
"I wish I did not have to ride on a
hot bus that shakes and is so slow.
I wish for a fast, cold ride."

Betty said, "Wish, wish, wish!
As soon as you sat down you started.
First the bus is too hot, then it
shakes, and now it is too slow.
It is hard to ride with a sister
like you."

Jill said, "When I get to the farm, I
know the first thing I'll do.
I'll go down to the lake.
That cold water will be good after
sitting on this hot, slow bus."

Soon the bus stopped for a wagon.
Jill looked at the wagon.

"That is Dad's wagon," said Jill.
"We don't have to ride on this hot,
slow bus."

Jill and Betty asked to get out of
the bus.
Then they ran to the wagon.

Dad said, "Why don't you girls
hop in the wagon?
I'll give you a ride to the house."

The girls hopped up in the wagon.

Then Dad said, "Here comes Mutt!
Mutt was just in the lake."

The dog hopped into the wagon.
The wagon started to go fast.
Mutt started shaking cold water
from the lake.
Cold water was flying on the girls.

Jill said, "Now this is a fine ride.
It is the fast, cold ride I
wished for!"

After the Fair

"You have a fine thick coat," said
Mark to the little sheep.
"I will show you at the next fair.
I'll call you Fluff, little sheep.
Right now I'll go get something good
for you to eat, Fluff.
You will be big and fat when it is
time for the fair."

"Did you hear that?" Fluff asked
Spot, a fat pig in the next pen.
"Mark will show me at the fair.
Mark can take you too.
We can both go to the fair."

The pig said, "Mark just shows sheep
at the fair.
He picks a fat sheep that looks good.
Mark will not show pigs at the fair."

"Then I don't want to go to the
fair," said Fluff, kicking the pen.
"I want to be at this farm with you.
I like having you to talk to.
This farm is where I want to be."

Soon it was time for the fair.
Fluff was big and fat.
Mark came to the sheep's pen.
He walked Fluff into a truck.
The truck started to the fair.

Fluff looked back at Spot's pen and
called, "Do something to help me!
I don't want to go to the fair!"

The pig called to the sheep, "I don't
know how to help you!"

Soon Fluff was at the fair.
She saw pens with fine farm animals.
Mark put Fluff into a pen.

A man saw Fluff and said, "I want
this sheep."

The man put Fluff into a truck.
Fluff did not want to go.
She started shaking and did not know
when the truck stopped at a farm.
But then the man came and helped
Fluff jump down from the truck.
A slow old sheep dog walked up.
The sheep dog licked Fluff.

The man said, "This is my dog, Homer.
Homer worked with sheep.
He is just not a happy dog.
He has no sheep to look after."

"But now I can look after you," Homer
said to the sheep.
"First I'll show you your new farm."

Fluff said, "I am on a new farm!
I like living on a farm.
I don't have Spot to talk to.
But I have Homer to look after me."

To be read by the teacher

I Held a Lamb

by Kim Worthington

One day when I went visiting,
A little lamb was there,
I picked it up and held it tight,
It didn't seem to care.
Its wool was soft and felt so warm—
Like sunlight on the sand,
And when I gently put it down
It licked me on the hand.

Reading
Bonus

The Fox and the Chick

One day a fat little chick wanted to go for a walk around the farm.
The little chick hopped along looking at the things on the farm.
Soon the chick was far from the hen house.
Then the chick met a fox.

"What a fine chick you are, and so
like your father," said the fox.
"I liked to chat with your father.
It made me happy just to talk to your
father and to hear your father sing.
Now that he is not here, I am lost.
Will you sing something for me as
your father did?
Please sing something.
Then please come to lunch with me.
Your father came to lunch with me."

Now, this little chick liked to sing,
and to hear what a fine chick it was.
So with a shake of its wing, it
hopped up and started singing.
But then the fox picked up the fat
little chick by its wing!

The farm dog saw the fox catch the
little chick.

"It looks like I have work to do,"
said the dog.

The dog chased after the fox.

"That dog is fast," the little chick
said to the fox.
"Tell the dog I want to go with you.
Then it will stop chasing us."

The fox started to tell the dog,
"This chick wants to go with me."

But as the fox was talking, it let go
of the little chick's wing.

The little chick ran from the fox.

Hopping back to the hen house, the chick said, "A chick who wants to live long will not sing for a fox!"

The dog chased the fox all the way to the fox's house.

Running from the dog, the fox said, "After this, I will not stop to chat when I am having my lunch!"

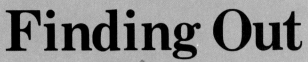

Section Three

Finding Out

107

The School Fair

Beth's Plan

Beth's school was having a fair soon.
Mr. Jay asked the girls and boys to
make things to show at the fair.
Beth did not know what to make.

"Mr. Jay wants us to plan something
good," said Beth.
"He wants us to learn from it.
But I don't have a plan."

Beth saw Ann making something with
two round cans.
She saw Ann cut a long rope and
put it into the cans.
Ann gave one can to Beth.
Next Ann picked up one can and walked
to the far side of the room.
Then Ann talked into the can.

Beth said, "I can hear Ann talking!
What she said into that can came
along the rope to this can.
Ann has planned something good."

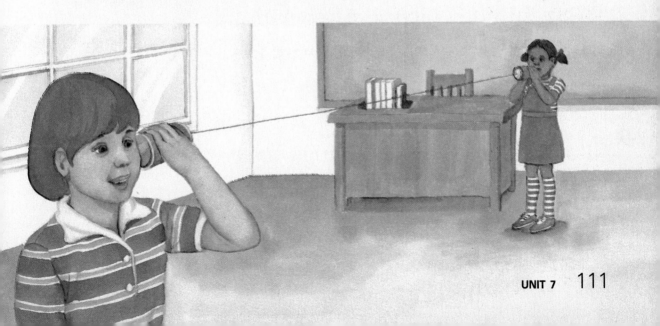

Beth saw Ed cut out a round shape.
He put paste on the picture he cut.

Ed said, "I am making a book of
pictures that have round shapes.
When I find a picture of something
with a round shape, I cut out the
picture and paste it into my book."

"Ed is learning which things have
round shapes," said Beth.
"What will I learn?"

Laura was cutting out a picture she made.
Beth saw Laura poke a pen into the picture and turn the picture fast.

Beth looked at Laura's picture when it was turning fast.
It did not look like the same picture.

Beth said, "Laura is learning what turning that picture with a pen poked into it does to the picture.
What will I learn?
I don't have much time to plan now."

Beth saw Bill cut some shapes out of paper and paste them together.

Bill said, "Look at all the paste, Beth.
Does this have too much paste on the sides?"

Beth said, "Yes, it does, Bill.
I'll get you some new paper to cut and paste."

Beth went to the table to get the paper.
Just then she saw a round ball of brown paper and some red paper blow from the table.

Beth saw both papers start to drop.
But they did not drop the same way.

Beth said, "The brown paper in the
shape of a round ball drops fast.
The red paper does not drop so fast.
I am learning that one paper can fall
fast and one paper can fall slow.
This is what I'll show at the fair!
But right now I'll show Bill.
Helping Bill helped me.
Now I have a plan for the fair."

Mike's Pet Snake

It was the day of the school fair.

"Is this your pet snake on the table,
Mike?" asked Judy.
"Does it sleep much?"

"It is my pet snake," said Mike.
"It sleeps so much that no one at the
fair wants to look at my pet snake."

Judy said, "I have a plan, Mike.
I'll tell the girls and boys that an
animal show is starting now.
They will want to see a show.
Can you put on an animal show?
You don't have much time to plan it."

"I can do it," said Mike.

So Judy called, "Step right up!
The animal show is starting."

Children came to see the show.

A boy asked, "Is it a picture show?"

"No, you will see a live animal, not
just pictures of one," said Judy.

Mike said, "The show will start now.
My snake is sleeping in its house.
I'll give my snake a little poke."

Mike poked his pet snake a little.
The snake moved to one side.

Then Mike said, "I have a fish for
my pet snake to eat.
My snake does not eat much.
This is all it needs for three days."

Mike dropped the fish into the
snake's water pan.
The snake moved to the side of the
pan and poked its head in the water.
Then the snake jumped at the fish.

A boy said, "The snake poked its head in and is eating all of the fish!"

"That is what my pet snake does," said Mike.
"If you look at the snake's side, you can see where the fish is."

"The snake's side is getting big behind the head," said a girl.
"That is where the fish is now.
This is a good show, Mike!"

The Snake

by Karla Kuskin

A snake slipped through the thin green grass
A silver snake
I watched it pass
It moved like a ribbon
Silent as snow.
I think it smiled
As it passed my toe.

Just For You

You can do the same thing that Beth did for the school fair.

1. Get a brown paper, a red paper, and a blue paper.

2. Make the brown paper into a round ball.

3. Drop the brown paper and the red paper at the same time.
   Does the brown one get down first?

4. Now drop the red paper and the blue paper at the same time.
Do both get down at the same time?

5. Now drop the blue paper and the brown paper at the same time.
Which paper drops all the way down first?

Just Animals

The Three Little Pigs

One morning Mother Pig called the
three little pigs together and said,
"Nosey, Pinky, and Curly.
It is time for you to go away and
learn to make your houses.
Don't let the wolf into your houses.
The wolf will want to eat you."

Mother Pig gave all three pigs a pat
on the head as the little pigs went
away the next morning.

"I want a straw house," said Nosey.
"Here comes a rabbit with some straw.
Rabbit, I want to make a straw house,
but I don't have any straw.
You have more straw than you need."

The rabbit gave Nosey some straw
and a pat on the head.
Nosey made a straw house.

But one morning the wolf came by
and said, "Little pig, let me in."

"No, I will not," said Nosey.

"Then I'll blow your house down,"
said the wolf, blowing.

"The wolf is blowing hard!
My straw house can not take any
more of this," said Nosey.
"I'll run away!"

So Nosey ran away from the wolf.

"I want a stick house," said Pinky.
"Here comes a dog with some sticks.
Dog, I want to make a stick house,
but I don't have any sticks.
You have more sticks than you need."
The dog gave Pinky some sticks
and a pat on the head.
Pinky made a stick house.

But one morning the wolf came by
and said, "Little pig, let me in."

"No, I will not," said Pinky.

"Then I'll blow your house down,"
said the wolf, blowing.

"The wolf is blowing hard!
My stick house can not take any
more of this," said Pinky.
"I'll run away."

So Pinky ran away from the wolf.

"I want a brick house," said Curly.
"Here comes a bear with some bricks.
Bear, I want to make a brick house,
but I don't have any bricks.
You have more bricks than you need."

The bear gave Curly some bricks
and a pat on the head.
Curly made a brick house.

Then Nosey and Pinky came by
calling, "A wolf is after us!
Please take care of us!"

Curly patted Nosey and Pinky on the
heads and said, "You can live here."

One morning the wolf came by and
said, "Little pigs, let me in."

"No, we will not!" said the pigs.

"Then I'll blow your house down,"
said the wolf, blowing.

The brick house did not fall down.
So the wolf went up on the house
to slide down into it.

Soon the wolf was sliding, sliding
down into the brick house.
But the three little pigs did not
care that the wolf was sliding.
The wolf was sliding into some hot
water that was on the fire.
The water was so hot that the wolf
jumped right out and ran away.
He did not come back any more.

The Baby Wolf

This **baby wolf** is taking a nap.
Soon he will want to eat.
The **mother wolf** will feed and take
care of the baby wolf.
All day long he will eat and nap in
the room that the mother wolf made.

One morning after his nap the baby
wolf starts patting and poking
something next to his mother.
It is a sister taking a nap.
The two of them play together.
The baby wolf learns that playing is
more fun than napping.

As days go by, the baby wolf finds
more little ones napping in the room.
He plays with them more and more.
As the baby wolf plays, he learns
what his family is like.

One morning as the mother feeds
the family, a big wolf comes in.
It is the **father wolf.**
He sees the five little ones and
wants to play with them.
He pokes and licks all five of them.

The baby wolf does not know this
wolf and hides behind his mother.
But she is happy to see the father.
So the baby wolf learns that he does
not need to hide from this big wolf.

One day after feeding the five little
ones, the mother wolf takes them
out of the room for the first time.
She takes all five to the father.
Then she walks away.

The baby wolf runs after his mother.
But he slides in some water and
falls on a stick.
The father wolf takes the baby wolf
back to the family.
The baby wolf learns that the father
wolf takes care of the family too.

A big wolf sees the five little ones
and comes to help the father wolf
take care of them.
Soon more big ones come.
The baby wolf learns that they all
live with his father and mother.
From now on they will all help feed
the five little ones in the family.

A big wolf will not feed the baby
wolf when the baby wolf gets big.
Then the little wolf will learn to
help catch any animals he eats.

A wolf eats big animals.
More than one wolf is needed to
chase and catch a big animal.
So the baby wolf will learn to work
together with his family.
But for now, the baby wolf will do
no more than play and nap.
And for now, the big ones will feed
and take care of the baby wolf.

The Farm Mouse and the City Mouse

Ben was a little brown farm mouse.
Alvin was a little brown city mouse.

Ben napped all day in his straw bed.
When the sun went down, he poked
his head out of his straw house.
He went out to find little round
seeds to eat.
Then he went back into his straw
house and napped in his straw bed.
Ben was happy.

One morning after a nap Ben called
Alvin up and said, "Come see me."

"I'll be happy to come," said Alvin.
"I'll learn what a farm mouse does."

The next morning Alvin put on his
brown coat and went to the farm.
He poked his head into Ben's straw
house.
Ben was happy to see Alvin.

Ben picked round seeds for Alvin.
He made Alvin a straw bed.
But the next morning after a nap,
Alvin put on his brown coat.

"Where are you going?" asked Ben.

"I am taking the train to the city,"
said Alvin.
"I don't wish to eat any more seeds.
I want more than the same little
round seeds that you feed me.
Why don't you come with me, Ben?"

Ben wanted to learn what living in the city was like.
He put on his brown hat and went with Alvin to the city that morning.

Alvin lived at the top of a big, wide house where a man and a woman and a pet cat lived.

"Does the pet cat chase you?" Ben asked Alvin.

"The pet cat does not know I live here," said Alvin.
"We can not let the family and the pet cat see us."

So with much care Ben and Alvin
walked along the side of a big room.
They both went into the room,
where they saw good things to eat.
Ben picked up something to eat.
Just then Alvin poked Ben.

"Here comes the man!" said Alvin.

Ben dropped what he was eating.
They ran away in the nick of time.
They did not get to eat any of the
good things they saw.

After a nap Ben and Alvin both
went back to the room where they
saw good things to eat.
Ben picked up something to eat.
Just then Alvin poked Ben.

"Here comes the woman!" said Alvin.

Ben dropped what he was eating.
They ran away in the nick of time.
They did not get to eat any of the
good things they saw.

After a nap Ben and Alvin both
went back to the room where they
saw good things to eat.
Ben picked up something to eat.
Just then Alvin poked Ben.

"Here comes the pet cat!" said Alvin.

Ben dropped what he was eating.
They ran away in the nick of time.
They did not get to eat any of the
good things they saw.

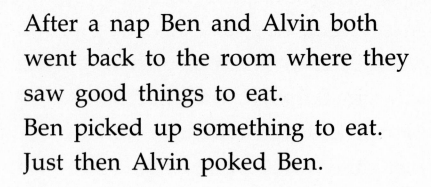

"That does it!" said Ben shaking.
"I don't want any more of this.
In the city you have more than little
round seeds to eat.
But you have to run away from a
man, a woman, and a pet cat!
Having to do that is not any fun."

So the next morning Ben put on his
brown hat and went to the farm.
Ben was happy.

I Wouldn't

by John Ciardi

There's a mouse house
In the hall wall
With a small door
By the hall floor
Where the fat cat
Sits all day,
Sits that way
All day
Every day
Just to say,
"Come out and play"
To the nice mice
In the mouse house
In the hall wall
With the small door
By the hall floor.

And do they
Come out and play
When the fat cat
Asks them to?

Well, would you?

Books to Read

Say Hello, Vanessa

by Marjorie Weinman Sharmat
No one comes to see Vanessa. But after she shows what she knows at school, things are not the same.

Toby in the Country, Toby in the City

by Maxine Zohn Bozzo
Two Toby's are in this book. They both do and like things that are the same.

Little Black Bear Goes for a Walk

by Berniece Freschet
Little Black Bear finds much to see and learn. And he finds something good to eat!

Pictionary

Can you read the signs?

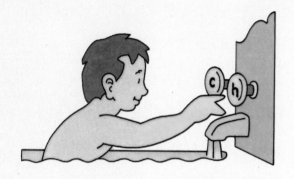

cold   hot

When you turn on the water, look for <u>cold</u> and <u>hot</u> (or <u>c</u> and <u>h</u>) to find out how the water will feel.

down   up

The words <u>down</u> and <u>up</u> tell you which way to go on steps.
The words <u>down</u> and <u>up</u> tell you which way you will ride too. You must not play here.

in   out

The words <u>in</u> and <u>out</u> tell you where to go.
The words <u>in</u> and <u>out</u> tell you which door to use, and which way a door will go!

keep out

Don't go in where you see <u>keep out</u>!

no running   don't run

If you run where you see this, you can fall.

slow—children

Drivers must go slow here. It is put where children walk or play, so drivers of trucks and cars will look out.

stop   stop here

The words <u>stop</u> and <u>stop here</u> are put up to tell cars and trucks to stop so you can walk.

Can you read pictures?

You can call home.

You can have a picnic here.

Do not ride your bicycle here.

You see this in a park or at a beach.

What I do for fun:

I <u>catch</u> a ball, or a boy or a girl.

I <u>chase</u> something, or some children.

I <u>hide</u> where it is hard to find me.

I <u>hop</u> in a good old game.

Things I learn at school:

I learn how to read.

I learn how animals live.

I learn how things work.

I learn how things are made.

I learn how to tell time.

Words we use many ways:

drop

A drop is a little ball of water. When you drop something, you let it fall.

ice

Ice is water that is so cold it is hard.
To ice a cake is to put a topping on it.

light

The sun gives light.
Lights help me see after the sun is down.
It is not hard to pick up something that is light.

park

I run and play in the <u>park</u>.
To <u>park</u> my wagon, I
move it and then stop.

pen

A <u>pen</u> is something I
can make a picture with.
A <u>pen</u> is something to
put animals in.

shake

I <u>shake</u> if I am cold.
I <u>shake</u> this to make
music.

Word List

The words below are listed by unit. Following each word is the page of first appearance of the word.